My Life Was Predestined by God

My Story

Roderick A. Johnson

ISBN 979-8-88751-092-7 (paperback)
ISBN 979-8-88751-093-4 (digital)

Copyright © 2023 by Roderick A. Johnson

All rights reserved. No part of this publication may be reproduced, distributed, or transmitted in any form or by any means, including photocopying, recording, or other electronic or mechanical methods without the prior written permission of the publisher. For permission requests, solicit the publisher via the address below.

Christian Faith Publishing
832 Park Avenue
Meadville, PA 16335
www.christianfaithpublishing.com

Printed in the United States of America

I want to dedicate this book to my darling wife. This wonderful woman, whom God has given me, has stood with me for the past sixty-one years, praying me through and forgiving me every time I messed up. It was God who chose and predestined our lives so that His sovereignty would be done, seeing that He is the final cause of everything.

I also want to dedicate this book to my children, especially my oldest, who stood with me throughout my ministry. They were deprived of many things so that others in poor situations in other countries would be blessed.

CONTENTS

ACKNOWLEDGMENTS

I must thank the people who stood with me through the years on the mission field in Guyana, Trinidad, Surinam, Dominica, Haiti, and right here on the streets of New Yok City and other states in the USA.

Proverbs 27:17 (NKJV) states, "As iron sharpens iron, so a man sharpens the countenance of his friend." These are some of my friends:

Apostle Johnny Washington (who is with the Lord)
Apostle Ira Davison
Dean Fay Carson (who is with the Lord)
Pastor C. R. Johnson (who is with the Lord)
Pastor Sam Ramphal
Pastor Michael Bacchus
Pastor Clayton Simpson
Evangelist Valerie Brocks (who is with the Lord)
Elder Mary Ann Gaddist
Evangelist Clara Garner
Elder Cynthia Middleton
Minister Colin Wronge
Pastor Earl and Barbara Mitchell
Mother Beatrice Brown (who is with the Lord)
Mother Doris Garner (who is with the Lord)
Pastor Enid Brotherson-Benjamin in Guyana
Pastor Wenneth Chapman in Guyana

Pastor Myrna Samuel in Guyana
Pastor Louralene Gouvetha in Guyana, ALM No.
8 Village, and all my leaders in Guyana

A special tribute to a sister, friend, and the best treasurer I could have asked for—the late Sister Rita Fraser, who was the wife of a wonderful brother in the church and mother of five children. Sister Fraser was also my power of attorney. She has gone home to be with the Lord.

I decree and declare in the name of Jesus Christ, God's richest blessings will continue to rest upon you all for your labor of love to others.

PREFACE

I offer this book with a sense of burden and fulfillment, but also with some hesitation.

My hesitation arises because I do not want to seem either boastful or condemning. My desire is to tell my story, hoping that everyone reading this book of my life may be blessed. I pray that they may know and understand that Jesus Christ is the same yesterday, today, and forever. And through the atoning sacrifice for the sins of humanity, Jesus has reconciled us to God, making us one again. My wife and I are truly blessed by God. Even while I was deep in sin, while living in Guyana, the Lord was protecting me. As you continue reading this book, you will see how much God loves me.

A Special Thanks

I have lived to see my eighty-first birthday, and by God's grace, on June 12, 2022, I will celebrate my eighty-second birthday. The Lord has been so good to me in many ways, especially the miracles he has performed in my life. I give God all the praise. And I thank my children and my darling wife, Lady Bernice Johnson, who spent days and nights throughout my illness with me, even in the hospital. My son Sheldon Johnson, whom God used at first, let the doctors know they were not signing any forms to release me from the machines. The Lord has called Sheldon home on December 21, 2019.

I thank my son Pastor Dwane Johnson. The spirit of God ordered him to squeeze my toes and ask for a response. My daughter, Pastor Sharon King, spent many nights sleeping in the waiting room in prayer. I thank my sons Roderick Johnson Jr. and Dexter Johnson for their support. I also thank my daughters-in-law. Nigele Johnson, who stayed day after day and told the doctors that they were not signing the release form. Sandra Johnson, Janet Johnson (a prayer warrior), and Samantha Johnson, who took turns with my daughter sleeping overnight in the waiting room and taking care of my wife during my absence. I thank my son-in-law, Minister Trevor King, for being there for my wife.

I am also grateful for my doctors: Dr. Richard Schwartz (my cardiologist) and Dr. Vincent Montoni (my primary care doctor). And gratitude to all the pastors and ministers who were praying me through. And thanks to all the doctors and nurses at the Winthrop Hospital emergency room and intensive care unit that God used to keep me alive. I love you all, and I am forever grateful.

MY LIFE WAS PREDESTINED BY GOD

My name is Roderick A. Johnson. At birth, the name Roderick A. Cameron was given me by my unwed parents, Ernest Cameron and Rosetta Johnson. That was on June 12, 1940, in Georgetown, Guyana, in South America (British Guyana).

Like many of the children in the sixties living in Guyana, I grew up extremely poor but "content." As a single parent, my mother worked extra hard to raise me, her only child at the time. Before I came of age for school, I can remember being held daily in my grandmother's arms as she took loving care of me while my mother worked. As I grew old enough for school, I had one school uniform and one pair of *yatim* shoes (Guyanese for sneakers on my feet). There were many days I went to school without lunch. At times, my friends and I would venture into the neighbor's yard just to steal fruit to have something to eat. In those days, every yard had a fruit tree.

When I was a twelve-year-old, I went to Kitty Assembly of God Church, where Harry Dass was the pastor. After hearing the preached message that Sunday, I felt God speaking to me. When the altar call was given, I went forward and accepted Christ as my Savior. I felt good. It was at this assembly that I met members on fire for Christ, as they held open-air street meetings. They were Sam, Sidney Ramphal, and Pearl.

The following week, I learned that Sam, Sidney, and Sister Pearl were going to an open-air meeting in Kitty. I was overly excited to join them (which they allowed), and from that day, I continued fellowshipping and going with them on every open-air meeting.

During the early years of my walk with Christ, I walked with a strong zeal of winning souls for Christ. However, at the same time, I was faced with teenage hormones that were unfamiliar to me. At sixteen, I had developed a fervent desire to have sexual encounters with girls. However, I experienced extreme difficulties in finding a partner due to my lack of confidence. My self-esteem had been damaged earlier in life from constant negative criticisms and verbal attacks that spurted out from those close to me. They were family members—all because I was born out of wedlock. My father and mother were not married, and in those days, in the minds of people, that was an awful thing.

My life took a leap backward when I met a woman who was sixteen years older than me at the time. I was persuaded to lose my innocence by this older woman, and my eyes were opened to an ungodly lifestyle. I was blinded by this new lifestyle and walked away from my Lord Jesus Christ.

My father was not a part of my life as I grew up. It was only my mother and grandmother until my grandmother passed on home to be with the Lord. Of course, my mother was the most loving and caring person I had ever known as I grew older.

When I stepped out of God's will, it was the worst thing I had ever done. I began searching, and since I was unable to keep a job, I joined the army (the "Guyana Defense Force"), where I stayed for three years and was discharged for fighting. I then found a job as a seaman (sailor) on a ferry ship in Georgetown. While on the ship, I met the girl of my dreams. I worked on the ship for five years before being dismissed. Once again, it was for fighting.

As I reiterate, my loving mother, even though she was not married to my father, worked hard to care for me, her only child at the time. She was insulted by family members as well as so-called friends. My mother took it all with her head up high and taught me what it took to be a man.

I was happy when God blessed my mother with a wonderful husband. Hubert Thompson was a fine gentleman. He became my stepfather and was more of a father to me than my biological father ever was. Out of their union came my brother, Blair, and my sister, Sandra Thompson.

I loved my mommy until God called her home at the age of ninety-three years old. Mommy was a darling. She is still in my heart until this day.

My Darling and I

I met the most beautiful girl I have ever seen while I worked on the ferry ship. Right away, I knew this girl would be my bride one day. (It was love at first sight.) Of course, she was only sixteen years old at the time, traveling back and forth to school on the ferry that I worked on as a sailor.

I was nineteen and working on the ferryboat when I saw the five-foot, four-inch young lady. She was wearing her school uniform. She weighed approximately ninety-five pounds and had her hair pulled back and braided. She had the face of an angel. My mind was blown! Each day, I would watch her as she crossed onto the ferryboat.

One day, I decided to run after her. I was extremely aggressive. As she crossed the ferry each day, I would take her kerchief out of her blouse pocket. I had about sixteen kerchiefs before she threatened to report me to the captain. Because of my aggressiveness, she was turned off from me. The captain insisted that I return her kerchiefs. Not too long afterward, she fell in love with me. We were truly in love as teenagers.

I was resiliently in love with her; therefore, I asked her parents for permission to visit her at her home in LaGrange. In the sixties, many parts of Guyana were undeveloped. We did not have lights on the streets; therefore, I took a taxi from the ferry to her house. Of course, after seven o'clock in the evening, the taxis had shut down, and there was no way for me to get back to the ferry. I needed the ferry to get back to my home in Georgetown.

It was four miles from Lagrange (the country area where my love lived) to the ferry, and it was extremely dark as time passed. After seven o'clock, it was very dark. I walked for many months through the dark streets to the ferry from her house. I needed to get to the ferry to go back home to Georgetown.

In 1958, I asked her to marry me. She was now seventeen years old, and I was twenty. The older siblings of my bride were very protective. They were highly educated and wanted the same for Bernice, my bride-to-be. They wanted the man that married Bernice to have an education as well.

Bernice's family started investigating my life as well as my family. When they found out that my mom was not married to my father and I was uneducated, I was forbidden to see Bernice again, nor was I allowed to come to Bernice's home.

Because of their threats, our love became stronger, and I was determined not to lose her. I was so happy when she told me that she felt the same. Whenever her parents would run errands or go to church, we would meet. There were many nights that I visited her and got stranded. When I checked the time, it was after seven o'clock, and the ferryboat had left because it was impossible for me to get a taxi to the ferry. Back in the fifties, the farmers would store bags of rice at the ferry storage. These would go the next day to the government barn. I used the rice bags for my bed on many nights. That was "crazy love."

Bernice turned seventeen during the year of her high school graduation. She desperately wanted me to be her guest at her high school prom, but her parents and brothers would not allow it. In fact, one of the brothers offered to take her himself. However, Bernice refused and missed the prom as well as her graduation because I was not allowed to be with her.

Moving On

The week following Bernice's graduation, we decided that no one would stop us. Early one morning, before anyone had awakened, I was at Bernice's house. I waited while she packed a bag. With her bag in her hand, she climbed through the window and jumped on my motorcycle, and we left. We traveled to a remote area in Guyana where we enjoyed each other for three days until the police came and questioned Bernice as to whether I had forced her to run away. She told them no and that she had left on her own, so they left us alone.

We understood the seriousness of our actions, so we left where we were staying and returned home to my mother's house. Before entering the house, my mother met us at the door, and the first words from her mouth were "the two of you are not living together in my house!" Of course, she allowed us to stay the night, but Bernice had to sleep in the room with my mother while I stayed in my room.

The next morning, my mother demanded that we take her to Bernice's parents' house. We were happy to do so. I loved my mother; she was always loveable but very strict and stern. She was no joke when it came to her son.

When we arrived at Bernice's parents' home, my mother went in while Bernice and I waited outside. An hour later, we were called in to join both of our parents. I was a bit anxious, however, especially when I scanned the faces of Mr. and Mrs. Vanier, Bernice's parents. They sat there for a while just looking at the two of us. Then, with a stern voice, Mr. Claude Vanier spoke. He said, "The two of you can get married."

I was so excited, I did not know how to act. Bernice was also happy to hear her dad giving permission for us to get married.

On December 16, 1961, we got married: Mr. and Mrs. Roderick Johnson. I was twenty years old, and Bernice was eighteen.

Bernice's parents, Mr. and Mrs. Vanier, were a wonderful couple with high morals. God had blessed them with fourteen children; however, when I met Bernice, four had died. And of the ten that were left, God had purposed that Bernice—the best of the ten daughters of Mr. Vanier—would be my bride.

When I think back on how Bernice's brothers banned me from their home because they did not feel I was good enough for their sister and how God had blessed us to be married, it is amazing. Before my father-in-law died, he said that I was the best son-in-law he had. Oh! I was thrilled. Those words made me feel good, knowing that God can take me from what I was and shape me into what I had become so that my father-in-law could have made that statement.

God bless Mr. and Mrs. Claude Vanier.

A Great Love for Children

My desire to have children was great. I do not know if it was the fact that I grew up without a father's love or something else, but I longed to have children. I did not keep this from my wife. I discussed having children with my wife and she agreed. Together, we desperately tried for five years. Thinking there might be a medical problem with one of us, we decided to see a doctor. After seeing the doctor, we got good news. Medically, we were both fine. We were just too anxious.

I know that God's hands were upon my life; I was just running from Him. Sam Ramphal became pastor and opened an Assembly of God church across the street from my home. Every Sunday, he would send a young man (John Cummings) to get me. The moment I saw him coming, I would run through the back door and disappear for the day.

After seven years of trying with no success, I was childless and frustrated. Then one day, the funniest thing happened. I never bought the papers before, but I just had this urge to buy a newspaper. There it was, in the headline of a story. A woman was giving up her children for adoption. Suddenly, I had to meet this woman.

I jumped on my motorcycle and eagerly began to search for her. The woman saw me coming as I approached the house. She opened the door and invited me in. I could not help from noticing the poor living conditions. I thought to myself, "This is poverty. And because of this, she is probably giving up her children."

She introduced herself as Ms. Medass. Right away, I asked about the children that I read about in the newspaper. I was told that the oldest girl was already adopted, but she had a boy (Dillon, three years old) and a two-year-old girl (Peola). As much as I wanted both children, Ms. Medass could not part from Peola. She needed to keep the girl with her.

I was ecstatic to finally have "a son." Both children were naked, so I took off my shirt, wrapped Dillon in it, and thanked Ms. Medass. I jumped on my motorcycle with Dillon and headed home to show my wife. I did not think to ask about the birth certificate.

Upon arriving home, I ran into the house holding this little boy (who was approximately twenty-five pounds) wrapped in my shirt. I will never forget the looks on the faces of my wife and my mother when they saw Dillon. Both my wife and my mother were surprised. Nevertheless, if that child would have come through any other means other than adoption, I would have been seriously hurt by my wife. My wife asked me, "Who is this child, and where is he coming from?"

I laughed then showed both my wife and my mother the newspaper article. I could see the relief on both their faces.

The following day, I took my wife to meet Dillon's mother, Ms. Medass, as she requested. After seeing the living conditions and Peola still not clothed, my wife agreed that we should once again ask for Peola. However, Ms. Medass could not bear to let Peola go. When I asked for the birth certificate for Dillon, I learned that he was not registered with the registry office. The way was made easy by God for my wife and me to go to the registrar's office to register our son, Dillon Alexander Johnson. We loved him so much, and my mother loved her grandson.

Every morning, I would take Dillon to play in the ocean. Since the water was salty, I thought it would make him tough and strong. Each day, I could not wait for my shift to end. In those days, there was much overtime, which I loved. But having our son, I would rush home to play with him. I took Dillon with me everywhere I went. It was me and Dillon on the motorbike, and at times, my wife would come along with us.

The Blessings That Followed

In 1967, the year after we had Dillon, my wife received an invitation to go to England. A few months later, she got another invitation to go to America. After talking about the invitations, we decided that we would accept the invitation to go to America. Both of us agreed that my wife would go to the USA first. We praised God for making the way, and we thanked God for my wife's aunt Janet Smith, who sponsored her. In 1968, my wife left Guyana to join her aunt in the United States of America while Dillon, my mother, and I remained in Guyana.

While in America, my wife worked for a Caucasian family who loved her, and in the same year, they became her sponsor. Later in 1968, my wife returned to Guyana to get her green card. After being influenced by her family and relatives in the United States of America, my wife returned to Guyana with the intention of leaving both me and my son, Dillon.

I thank God that he had already predestined our lives.

The Year of New Beginnings

Early one morning in October 1968, my wife and I went to the American Embassy to get her green card so that she could become a permanent citizen of the United States of America. I was not allowed to go in for reasons I did not understand at the time. However, the officer that was interviewing my wife noticed in the papers that she was married and asked where her husband was and why she was not filing for her husband as well. My wife told him that she was unaware that she could file for me at that time and was planning to do so later. The officer instructed her to get the proper application, fill it out, and return after lunch. That made my wife incredibly angry.

When Bernice came out of the office, she was furious. I did not know why at first, but she took my hand, pulled me across the street, and said to me, "I had no intentions of taking you back with me to the United States. That is why I did not put your name on the application. But the officer said I must put your name on the application and return after lunch."

Now my wife, who was about ninety pounds and five feet tall, looked me in the face and told me what she would and would not do should I come with her to America. I engaged in many things and practices that Bernice did not approve of in Guyana. I cannot repeat her exact words, but she made me promise that I would change if I wanted to go with her. I made her a promise, but in my heart and mind, I had other thoughts.

GOD'S PLAN FOR US IN THE USA

It was during the winter months in the USA, so we decided to leave Dillon in Guyana with my mother until we got settled. We arrived in the USA in October 1968. It was cold, but I loved the change of weather. My wife's aunt Winnie found an apartment for us on Washington Avenue in Brooklyn, New York. The apartment was on the fourth floor, and I did not like the idea of my wife having to climb four flights of stairs every day. Never have I seen so many apartments in one building. I at once told Aunt Winnie that we would not continue to stay there. We stayed for one week and found another apartment in a two-family house, which we loved. Our proprietors were genuinely nice, and we loved the area. In March 1969, my mother and son, Dillon, joined us.

Amazingly, I was offered a security guard's job at Brooklyn Jewish Hospital the first day we arrived in Brooklyn. It was a respectable job for me at the time. Then I was astonished. On my first day on the job, God sent a nice little lady, Mother Lillian Clark, to tell me how much Jesus loved me. Mother Clark was about five feet tall, the same as my wife. She talked about Jesus for a while before noticing that I was not responding. Then she gave me a tract and invited me to her church, "God's Battalion of Prayer."

Two weeks later, I saw Mother Clark, and she saved my life. God used her to rescue me. (Bad habits never die on their own.) I had just received my first paycheck after working two weeks. I cashed the check that day, and instead of leaving my money at home, I brought the money with me to work. That night, while making my rounds checking the building, I stumbled on some workers gambling, playing cards. I was invited to join them and ended up losing all the money I had. I did not have one dime left to go home with.

I went home the following morning to face my wife with a lie. I told my wife that I fell asleep at the desk at work, and my wallet was stolen. I then borrowed some money from Aunt Winnie. I went to the store and bought a switchblade knife. That night, I went to work with the intention of getting my money back. I somehow knew that I had been cheated. The men that invited me into their game had taken me as fresh meat because I had just arrived in town from a foreign country.

I purposely arrived fifteen minutes early for my eleven-to-seven shifts. Just as I punched in my time card, I saw Mother Clark. She looked at my face and asked, "Son, what is wrong? I see something terrible in your face."

I replied, "Nothing, Mother."

She then said, "Don't tell me nothing. I know what I see."

I really do not know how this happened, but tears began to flow, and I told her everything. Mother Clark took the knife from me and prayed with me. She told me to go to work and that I was going to have a good night. I hugged and kissed Mother Clark and went on my way to my department. Because of the prayers and the encouraging words from Mother Clark, I forgot about the men, the money, and the things that I had planned to do. I did have a good night, and I never played cards again.

The second week in November, I received my second paycheck from the hospital. Because my wife worked in New Jersey, she only came home on weekends, usually on Saturdays. I decided to go to Manhattan that Friday evening since I was off that weekend. Little did I know that God was setting me up.

I took the train to Penn Station, and as I came up the steps onto Seventh Avenue, a Chinese restaurant caught my eye. I went upstairs to the restaurant at Thirty-Third Street and Seventh Avenue. To my surprise, I saw three friends from Guyana. The restaurant was crowded, and we were the only Black people there. I honestly felt important, being surrounded by so many Caucasians. Being in

America one month, I thought to myself that I had never sat in a restaurant with Caucasian people while in Guyana.

My friends and I were enjoying each other's company while we ate, when we saw three Black American bandits come into the restaurant with guns. Holding their guns, the bandits demanded that everyone empty their pockets, rings, watches, and all wallets on the table. I saw a few people get pistol-whipped because they did not want to give up their possessions. My friends and I sat in the far rear of the restaurant. All I could think of was I was not losing my green bills again, so as my friends emptied their pockets, I began putting my green bills into my socks while they were not looking. I mixed my coins with my friends' money on the table. Then just as one of the bandits approached our table, I heard a voice saying "freeze!" I looked and saw a police officer with his gun drawn. The bandit who was at our table dragging off the money turned around with his gun in his hand. The police officer saw us at the table sitting next to the bandit and opened fire. Fearfully, we scrambled under the table. I did not remember when I prayed last, but at that moment, I began praying. As I prayed, I began to remember some of the things Mother Clark said to me, and at that moment, I promised God that if he would spare my life, I would serve him until I die.

When the shooting was over, the bandit that was next to our table was shot in the forehead. He died lying on the floor next to me and my friends. I was frozen, and the police officer helped me up as he began questioning us. I was so afraid and frozen that I was no help to the police officer at that time. We were taken to the police precinct where, after several hours, I was able to tell them what I had seen. The police sergeant at that time sent us home in a police car.

When I got home, I was still in shock. I began smoking a cigarette, trying to calm myself. After a while, I called my wife, who was still at work. I told her what had happened, and she was quite upset. However, all I could think about was finding Mother Clark's church: God's Battalion of Prayer. Mother Clark was the church mother who had invited me before. Since it was a Friday night, I had to wait until Sunday morning to attend a church service.

I was so excited to go to church, I woke up at 4:00 a.m. to get dressed. At 5:30 a.m., I was on my way, searching for Mother Clark's church. I was disappointed when, at 6:30 a.m., I was still searching and could not find the church building.

I felt lost until I saw a lady dressed all in white. Thinking she might know of the church, I asked her if she knew where God's Battalion of Prayer Church was. She replied, "No, but I am going to church, and you are welcome to come with me."

The Day My Life Was Changed

It was a frigid winter day. After searching for hours for God's Battalion of Prayer Church, I met a stranger who invited me to go with her to church. I accepted the invitation, not knowing it was all in God's plan. This lady dressed in white was sent by God.

The church was at the corner of Classon Avenue and St. Marks Street in Brooklyn. The church service began at 7:00 a.m., and as I sat there in the back of the church, it seemed as if the pastor was talking directly to me as he preached. He preached about my entire life, and it was devastating. It was as if he knew me, and this was my first time ever sitting in one of his services. I found myself shaking as tears ran down my face as I sat there on the bench. When the pastor made the altar call at the end of his sermon, I ran to the altar crying, asking God to forgive me for all my sins. I again promised God that I would serve him for the rest of my life.

I was surrounded by the mothers and brothers in the church as they all were praying over me. I accepted Jesus Christ into my heart and committed my life to him from that day onward. I left that church feeling good.

When I got home, I sat on my bed, thinking. I could not believe I was saved. I was a heavy smoker during those days. As I sat on the bed, I took a cigarette out and lit it. But as I made that first puff on the cigarette, it tasted bitter in my mouth. I immediately put it out and lit another one. It was also bitter, and right there, a voice said to me, "I have taken the taste of cigarettes out of your mouth."

That was the last time a cigarette entered my mouth. To God be the glory. I began to praise God, my Lord, and my Savior for my deliverance. I had been a heavy smoker for fourteen years.

On the next day, Monday, I went to work, and the first person I saw was Mother Clark. I began to tell her of my experience, and she began to praise God openly in the hospital. I could see the excitement on her face. Once again, my tears were flowing; but this time, they were tears of joy. My life changed, and so did my job status.

That same week, I felt the Lord saying to me, "Go to Citibank." It was at 111 Wall Street in Manhattan. I got up that Thursday morning and got dressed. This was my first time wearing a tie in a long time. Nevertheless, I put on my best suit and tie. I went into Citibank and was directed to the employment office on the eleventh floor.

I dropped out of school when I was thirteen to help my mother. Therefore, when I went for the interview, I was extremely nervous because I did not have a high school education. I was afraid of failing whatever test I would have to take. When I was given the test, I was able to do all the math because math was my best subject when I did go to school. When the examiner returned, I had only finished half the test. I was in that room for hours. She took the papers from me, looked at them, and said, "You are slow, but you look smart. Report to work on Monday. Go to the third floor. They will be expecting you."

I was thankful for how God used this woman to open the door for me. She was a blessing.

I was so anxious to visit Mother Clark's church that I went back to the hospital to get the address. The following Sunday, I visited with Mother Clark at her church. The people were extra friendly, and they made me feel welcome. I wanted my wife to be with me, but she was at work in New Jersey at that time. She only came home every other weekend. When I called to tell her I had accepted Jesus Christ as my Lord and Savior, my wife laughed at me and replied, "You got saved. I don't believe it. I will be coming home next weekend to see this change in you."

The next weekend, my wife came home, and that Sunday, she joined me in church. My wife, Bernice, accepted the Lord Jesus Christ as her Savior. It was a turning point for both of us. Within one month, both of us received Christ in our lives.

I reported to work at Citibank as I was directed and went to the third floor, where I met my section head. He was a very nice man whose name was Richie. He directed me to my desk and gave me some work and began to teach me. He explained that I would be a stock dividend clerk. Can you imagine what was going through my mind? I began to blot out all negative thoughts and said to myself, "I can do this."

After one month, I became a professional stockbroker. To God be the glory. I worked overtime, and to my surprise, I was making more money than I had expected. I was promoted three times in five years. It was all God's doing.

A New Life in Christ

We met some lovely people at the Battalion of Prayer, the church where we joined Mother Clark. Just to name a few, we met Brother and Sister Kenneth Ware, Brother Ralph Byrd, Sister Morris, Mother Wronge, Sister Barbara Mitchel, Brother and Sister Michael Bacchus, and many more.

Brother Byrd was attending the Manhattan Bible Institute, where Dr. Edward H. Boyce invited me many nights to go with him. I accepted the invitation and joined Dr. Boyce. I enjoyed sitting in the classes that year. The Christian Workers class and the Evangelism class were the first two classes I visited and enjoyed.

As 1969 was ending, I knew in my heart that God's spirit was leading me to register for the 1970 classes. However, I was greatly concerned about my ability in reading, which was not one of my favorite subjects. Nevertheless, I got the courage to see Dr. Boyce. I introduced myself and told him that I would like to attend Bible school the next year (1970), but I did not know how to read and spell properly. Dr. Boyce said, "Son, you are at the right place. There are instructors who will help and guide you."

Dr. Boyce introduced me to Dr. Clarence R. Johnson and Dr. Ira Davison. They were instructors. Dr. Johnson was called Dr. C. R. Johnson. He took a special interest in me because we had the same last name. I was happy with my new brothers, whom I also called my friends.

In 1970, Brother Byrd and I traveled to Bible school every week. The first course I took was Evangelism, and I loved it. I will always thank Dr. Sam Ramphal. I believe the seeds that were sown into my life during my early age did not die. God was working in my life even when I was deep in sin. I know Jesus loved me then, and he still loves me now.

Before I started Bible school in 1969, my wife and I were taken to Staten Island to be baptized. After being baptized, I remember telling my wife that she would be pregnant on her birthday, which was September 21, 1969. Lo and behold, my wife was pregnant with our first biological son.

For the first seven years of our marriage, as bad as we wanted children, we did not have a child until we adopted Dillon in 1967. But here in 1969, after I gave my life to Christ, God showed me that my wife would be with child on her birthday. Just as God promised, my wife was pregnant on her birthday. And on May 31, 1970, our son Sheldon Alexander Johnson was born. I prayed for another child, a girl, but God blessed us with another boy in October 1971, Dwayne A. Johnson. Again, I prayed for a girl and was blessed with two more sons: Roderick Jr. in 1976 and Dexter in 1977.

I praise God for all my sons. I loved them dearly, but I continued praying for the girl that I wanted. Early one morning in 1978, I got a call from my cousin in Guyana who, at that time, had a financial problem. She had a three-year-old daughter that she was unable to care for, and she wanted her daughter to have a better life. She called to ask my wife and me to adopt her three-year-old daughter. I quickly replied yes, and at once, we began the paperwork.

When the adoption paperwork was completed, we sent my mother back to Guyana because all the adoption paperwork was managed there. We named our daughter Sharon Abigale Johnson. My mom and our daughter arrived on June 12 of 1969, just in time for my birthday. What a blessing! I shouted, "Hallelujah! Hallelujah! Hallelujah!" God has blessed us with the family we wanted. My wife and I purposed in our hearts that we would be the best parents we could be. Our desires were that all our children would grow up in a warm and caring environment, loving each other, and the adoption would never be mentioned among them until they were older enough and ready. They would graduate high school and go to college.

Again, God granted us our desires for the children; they had a genuine love and closeness. My wife and I would watch in amazement as the two eldest boys defended their sister, and their sister, Sharon, was defending and fighting for the two youngest, Roderick Jr. and Dexter.

On three separate occasions when I thought Dillon was mature enough and of age, I took him with me to Guyana with the intention of having him meet his biological mother. However, on each trip, we were unable to find her. Dillon was eighteen on the third trip, and when we could not find her, Dillon said to me, "Dad, I do not wish to search for her anymore. Take me home." I was still carrying the newspaper article that led me to my son's adoption, but when my son said to me that he did not want to search for her, I at once discarded the article and took my son home.

When Sharon was seventeen years old and getting ready to attend college, her biological mother was visiting the USA. When she approached me to get permission to meet my daughter and let my daughter know who she was, I straightforwardly refused. I had never talked to Sharon about her being adopted because of the impoverished situation she was in when I found her. I did not want to take the chance of Sharon changing her mind about college after meeting her biological mother. I was not about to let anything hinder my baby's progress. I then suggested to the biological mother that I would let Sharon know when she was twenty years old and when she graduated from college. And at that time, we told her about the adoption and that her biological mother wanted to meet her. We also told our sons of the adoption of Sharon and Dillon. Everyone was happy, and they never held it against me or my wife.

We let Sharon's biological mother know that Sharon had graduated from college and that she was welcome to meet her. She was grateful. She understood why I had to do what I did, and today, they have a beautiful mother-daughter relationship. Our daughter, Sharon, is now married to a God-fearing man—Trevor King, a minister. They have two sons: Elijah and Ezekiel. Sharon is now a youth pastor, and her husband is a minister of the Gospel of Jesus Christ.

In 2019, I contacted a close friend whom I consider a brother. I asked him to help find Mrs. Medass, Dillon's biological mother. Three weeks later, I received a call from my friend Ernist, informing me that he had found one of Dillon's sisters. He then gave me the information to reach her. I called to ask her a few questions to assure myself that she was the right person. After my inquiry, I was satisfied, and I released the information to Dillon. Dillon was excited to know that he had other siblings. He got connected with all his siblings, and he also found out that his biological mother had died. Dillon is now a pastor. He is married to a mighty woman of God, Janet Credle. Together, they have three children: Amanda, Kayla, and Dillon Jr.

All our children took part in ministry at an early age. After joining God's Battalion of Prayer and graduating from my first course in Bible school (Evangelism), we began the ministry of evangelism in our church. The pastor appointed me to be the evangelist of our church. We became engaged in street meetings. God blessed us with young men, singers, musicians, and preachers on the evangelist team. As of today (January 12, 2022), all the people God blessed us with are pastors or ministers of the Gospel of Christ. Let me name a few:

- Pastor Michael Bacchus
- Pastor Roland Grant
- Pastor Conrad Stapleton
- Pastor Lincoln Brown
- Elder Colin Wronge
- Elder Joseph Higgins

My son Dillon was the drummer on the street team when he was ten years old. He is now Pastor Dillon Johnson. As for the rest of my sons, Minister Sheldon Johnson is married to a godly woman, Sandra White. Together, they have one son, Joshua. The Lord called Sheldon home when he was forty-nine years old on December 21, 2019. He is missed. Our first biological son, Dwayne Johnson, married Nigele Madu. He is the father of seven children. As for our last two sons, Roderick. Jr. is the father of two sons and one daughter. And Dexter married Samantha Savory. Together, they have two daughters. My last two sons keep me on my knees. I believe that they will receive salvation because God has promised me they will.

This walk with God has not been easy. My wife was truly given to me by the Lord because I could not have made it this far if it had not been for the Lord at my side and my wife—a great and wonderful woman of God—standing with me throughout the good and the troubled times.

In 1977, Mother Lillian Clark became the pastor of God's Battalion of Prayer Church, but she never had the privilege of seeing the completion of the building because the Lord had called her home. It was a beautiful building on Linden Boulevard in Brooklyn, which we bought.

Immediately after the completion of our new building, there were many disagreements about who would take over as pastor. Everyone knew that Michael Bacchus was assigned to become the pastor, but there were some who challenged him for the office of pastor. It was becoming very ugly, even though Michael Bacchus was the most qualified. It was time for me and my family to find another fellowship. I saw where this was heading. The fighting for that position would only get worse, and so it did.

My friendship with Reverend Clarence Johnson of the Manhattan Bible Institute led me to join his church, the Tabernacle of Prayer, where he was the assistant pastor to Apostle Johnnie Lee Washington, the founder and senior pastor of the Tabernacle of Prayer for All People in Jamaica, New York. This was all new for me, leaving a church with seventy-five members and joining a church with approximately seven hundred members, which grew a little over five years to three thousand members.

I met Apostle Washington on the streets of Brooklyn as the street team I led was conducting street meetings. Most Saturdays, Apostle Washington led a street meeting on Fulton Street (also in Brooklyn). When he had finished his street meeting, he would come over to our street meeting in Albee Square in Downtown Brooklyn. This was a great and wonderful service we had on Albee Square. Many souls were saved at that location.

I was blessed to spend three years studying at the Manhattan Bible Institute; but when Rev. C. R. Johnson became the dean of the Tabernacle of Prayer Bible Institute, he asked me to go with him. I accepted his invitation and finished my years of study at the Tabernacle Bible Institute. It was here at the Tabernacle of Prayer where I realized that the Holy Spirit was my best teacher, and that was utterly amazing.

After spending one year at TBI (Tabernacle Bible Institute) and three years at MBI (Manhattan Bible Institute), Dr. C. R. Johnson asked me to teach the Evangelism and Christian Workers classes. I was shocked and, at the same time, excited for the challenge, for I knew that God had chosen me for a purpose. I had never told anyone at the Tabernacle of Prayer about my inabilities, and one day, the Lord spoke to me. He said, "Stop thinking about your inabilities. You can do all things through me who strengthens you."

And that was it. I moved forward with those words in my spirit. Many of my students thought I was a college graduate, and I allowed them to assume that. But at the same time, I was studying extremely hard, knowing I was teaching college students.

Apostle Washington took a strong interest in me. Remember, we met when I was conducting street Services, so he knew of my ministry. Six months later, I went to Apostle Washington and told him I would like to start a street team to minister under his umbrella with his permission. His words to me were "What took you so long?"

The following Sunday, from the pulpit, Apostle Washington made an announcement that I would be starting an evangelistic street ministry, and I was looking for team members. After morning worship, those who were interested in joining the street ministry were asked to meet me across the street at the Tabernacle Bible Institute.

I went over to the Tabernacle Bible Institute building expecting to see about ten to twelve people. To my amazement, there were over one hundred people waiting. I was overly excited, seeing so many who were interested in working for the Lord. Among the one hundred people, there were great anointed singers and musicians. I perceived that many of them were Bible school students. I immediately began to thank God for giving me the gift and ability to bring out the gifts that were in his people. God has placed in every person he has chosen a gift to minister, even though I did not know the ministry gift God had placed in me.

Our street team became more powerful than ever. The Lord was with us. We were having street services in Times Square in New York City every Saturday during the summer months. In every street service, we saw many people who had accepted Jesus Christ as their Savior.

Apostle Washington assigned the street ministry to be forerunners for the upcoming church conventions. We began traveling to other states, sharing the gospel in the streets a week before the church convention would begin. Many souls were saved, healed, and delivered in the streets of Raleigh, North Carolina, during our first convention.

I remember one year, we were in Raleigh, North Carolina, having a street meeting at lunchtime. Many people stopped after hearing our singers and our musicians, and some among the audience were singing along as our singers sang. There was a Caucasian man in the crowd who had just left the courthouse, where he was filing for a divorce. He heard the gospel message and came forward to give his life to Christ. Many followed him, giving their lives to Christ. That man went back to court and stopped his divorce proceeding.

During the night of the convention, that same man came to the service asking for me. The ushers escorted him to the front and introduced him to Apostle Washington. He told Apostle Washington what had happened to him at the meeting the day in Raleigh. Apostle Washington convinced the man to share this testimony. After he gave his testimony, the body of believers, about three hundred people, went up into a high praise and dance. That man had the victory. To God be the glory.

Dr. C. R. Johnson's time was up at the Tabernacle of Prayer for All People, and God directed him to establish a ministry in Brooklyn, New York: the "Brooklyn Tabernacle." Again, he asked me to go with him, but this time, God did not give me his approval to leave the Tabernacle of Prayer for All People, so I remained there.

Dr. Fay Carson became the dean of the Bible school. She was a mighty woman of God and was strong in the faith. Dean Carson called me into her office one day and told me to prepare to teach. I was already teaching, so I said to myself, "Where is she going with this?" Before I could answer her, she assigned five classes to me to teach every week. Because of all my studying to teach each week, I began to grow increasingly in the Lord. I really fell in love with the Word of God.

Some of the college students in my class began planning for me to speak at their colleges. I accepted all the invitations that were offered. Now, as I look back over my life and see where God has brought me from and what he had put in me that I know not of, I can praise him all day long. He has been so good to me.

There is another brother who had a significant impact on my life—Apostle Ira Davison, whom I met at the Manhattan Bible Institute. Apostle Davison was the host pastor for the upcoming convention in New Orleans. He also was the pastor of the New Orleans Tabernacle for All People when Apostle Washington sent the street team to New Orleans as forerunners for the church.

The night that we arrived in New Orleans, we checked into our hotel and had a restful night's sleep. We woke up to discover that someone had stolen all our instruments from the van. The church of New Orleans, along with our street team, began to pray. We asked God to let the thieves return our instruments. After the prayer, we all went looking for our instruments.

The Holy Spirit led two of our mothers into a yard where they found our instruments. It was the house of the person who stole them from our van. Oh, what praise and worship we rendered to God after the instruments were recovered! We then loaded our truck and began driving around, searching for a spot, trusting the Holy Spirit to direct us to the right spot to hold our street meeting because we did not know anything about New Orleans. As always, we relied on the Holy Spirit to find the right spot for our street meeting when we traveled out of state.

The Holy Spirit directed us to an apartment project with an open space where we were able to set up for street meetings. We quickly began setting up our instruments for service. Of course, we did not know the name of the project, nor did we know the project's reputation. I had the musicians set up the instruments while the team members divided themself into small groups and went into the apartment building, giving out gospel tracts and inviting people to come out to our service. The things that we experienced as we entered the hallways of the complex would have made an ordinary person run and get far away from those projects. But we were not just ordinary people; we were anointed by God for this mission. Praise God.

As the team walked through the building handing out gospel tracts, there were bloodstained clothes on the floor of the hallways of the apartments. We were warned of the shootings and stabbings every week. The police had left them alone, but God did not leave them. He sent witnesses that they might receive salvation.

We continued as planned. The team began to praise and worship God, the singers singing and the musicians playing. Then one of our singers, Sister Roslyn Loncke, took the lead, and soon the other singers began singing "Take Me Back." The people began coming out of their apartments with chairs and filled the grounds where we were.

There were approximately fifty people there, while many others were sitting at their windows enjoying the service. Evangelist Valerie Brocks preached that evening, and many that stood and sat around gave their lives to God. It was an evening to be remembered. We found out that the name of that project was Saint Bernard, and it had a notorious reputation. We were told later that no outsiders would dare go there, not even the police! The people were afraid for their lives, and there was evidence of violence in the project in those days, but God turned it around after the three days that we spent with God there. Apostle Davison was happy with the success of the street team. He invited the team back to New Orleans for two consecutive years afterward.

When we returned to New York a few weeks later, we were having a service at Forty-Fourth Street and Broadway in Manhattan. A beautiful Caucasian lady came up to me and told me that after we left New Orleans, the Lord led her and a few others to open a soup kitchen in the Saint Bernard Projects and that it was a true blessing to the families that lived there. I was incredibly happy to hear of her newfound ministry, and it was truly God's doing.

When Apostle Davison, his wife, and children relocated to New York, they were a part of the Tabernacle of Prayer family in Jamaica, New York. Apostle Davison is an extraordinary man of God; he loves souls. Together with some members of our street team, he spent one week in Wolford Square in Trinidad, W. I. Apostle Davison preached every night. We also traveled with a team to Barbados, W. I., Guyana, and Surinam—and again back to Trinidad and Guyana. On these trips, we saw many souls saved. This was all God and not about us. At some of our crusades, I may have preached, but I knew that those with me were anointed to carry the word while I did the organizing and planning, giving way for God to bring the gifts and potential out of those who were traveling with me. I was so blessed to have some great anointed preachers and singers and musicians to carry forth this powerful gospel of Jesus Christ.

I thank God for Apostle Johnny Washington, who trusted me with seventy-five members of his congregation to travel all over the USA, carrying the gospel of Jesus Christ. I also thank God for our street evangelical team. These people followed me without questioning my decisions. This team was regarded as second to none by Apostle Washington and many other pastors who saw the power of God moving in our midst.

On Forty-Fourth Street and Broadway, a man with a gun was threatening our team because our sisters wore a white headpiece during our fifty-day consecration. Another miracle we experienced was when we were at Forty-Second Street between Broadway and Seventh Avenue in New York City. As our meeting was in session, a heavy rain came down, but the rain fell on the west side of Seventh Avenue and east of Broadway. Where we were between Broadway and Seventh Avenue, the rain did not fall. People from both sides of the streets ran over to where we were. Praise the Lord! The street team was truly anointed by God, and our singers and musicians were the bait to draw the people in.

Each time we went out to minister on the streets during the summer months, we got a greater crowd, and we never took a Saturday off unless it rained. Every Saturday when we were not out of state, we had a double hitter. At 12:00 noon, we ministered at Jamaica Avenue and Merrick Boulevard at the side of the church building, and at 6:00 p.m., we ministered at Forty-Fourth Street and Broadway or Forty-Second Street between Broadway and Seventh Avenue.

The Bible speaks of iron sharpened iron. Today, 60 percent of our street team members are ministers of the gospel of Jesus Christ. Some are pastors, bishops, and evangelists. As for me, God has used me to be the planter of two churches in Guyana, and as of today (February 1, 2022), they are growing tremendously. All praises and glory to our God.

Thank you, street team of the Tabernacle of Prayer for All People.

A Special Call

On April 22, 1986, Apostle Johnny Washington went home to be with our Lord. At that time, the Lord told me to go to Guyana, not as the previous times to evangelize but to start a ministry. That same year, my wife and I traveled to Guyana to do exactly what God told me to do. I knew our exact assignment; it was to establish a home for children.

The Lord was with us as my wife and I arrived in Guyana. The next day, we went searching for a home to rent. The Lord led us to a store where we began to speak about our Lord Jesus Christ. While in the store talking to the owner, we began to tell him of our desire to find a home for children. He told me that he had a building, and he would be glad to rent it to us. I said, "Thank you, sir. It will be a blessing to many children." The rental price was $30,000 per month in Guyana currency (at that time, it was equivalent to $15 US currency). A contract was signed three days later, and we paid four months in advance.

A soon as we opened and furnished the home, the Welfare Department (I spoke to them a few days before) called to inform me that they had five children for us. These children were siblings, all girls. Now we needed a housemother to take care of our girls.

The Lord directed us to a woman of God whom we met years before when we came to Guyana with a team. Her name was Pastor Enid Brotherton. At that time, she was pastoring a young ministry. Again, the Lord spoke plainly to me: "Tell Pastor Brotherton the

Lord said she was to leave where she was and take over the home for children."

We registered our ministry under the name Abundant Life Ministries Guyana. I said to Pastor Brotherton, "I have delivered the message. God will have to speak to you himself." Before we left, we prayed for Pastor Brotherton-Benjamin.

My wife and I hired a housemother and returned to New York. Within three months, the Welfare Department in Guyana sent us four more girls. We now had nine girls in the home. The girls' ages ranged from six years to nine years old. They were all of school age.

The Lord had blessed us with a limousine business, and we were making good money. My wife and I were able to send $550 every month to cover the rent and the house expenses.

The following year (1988), I received a letter from Pastor Brotherton-Benjamin stating that the Lord spoke to her, and she was ready to do his work in Abundant Life Ministries. In 1988, Pastor Enid Brotherton-Benjamin became a part of our ministry, and she assumed the headship of our ministries in Guyana.

Pastor Benjamin had always been a sanctified woman of God. When we met, she was single at the age of forty-five and was determined to live her life for God. She was a graduate of the Assemblies of God Bible College and was also a Bible school teacher. My wife and I were happy to have her with us because there were few trustworthy people when it came to position and money. We trusted Pastor Benjamin to be our power of attorney. It was the beginning of something great.

That same year, a mother came to our children's home with two boys and a girl, asking for our help. We received the three children after the applications were completed. Right across the street from our home was a church (210 Assembly of God Church) where Pastor and Mother Gittens were pastoring. I was grateful that our children had a church to attend, and Pastor Gittens and his wife were more than pastors to our children. They became their grandparents. They loved my wife and me as well as our children.

On every visit to Guyana, we were treated like royalty. Mother Gittens had my wife, myself, and my team attend a special dinner one evening. The dinner included dessert, which was cake and homemade ice cream.

In November 1989, Mother Gittens called me to ask if we would help another family, someone she knew had children but no place to live. One day before I got the call from Mother Gittens, our housemother, Sister Shulves, died and was buried. After I consulted God for another housemother, I spoke to Pastor Benjamin, and then I told Mother Gittens, "Yes, we will take the family. But the woman will have to be the housemother."

The next day, a van pulled up to our home. The father and mother came into the house and introduced themselves as Mr. and Mrs. Cox. I will never forget that day because, after the parents gave their introduction, the children followed them. There were eight beautiful children. With this family, we would then have twenty children and two adults.

Mrs. Cox became the housemother that evening; she was an exceptionally good cook. The other children that were already in the home were sad because they missed Sister Schultz. But before long, they fell in love with the new housemother, who treated all the children equally (which was my main concern). Brother Cox was a mechanic, and he asked my permission to do some mechanical work at the home. He had the space, so I gave him my permission. God had blessed us with a big and beautiful home, and the children were happy.

Brother Cox and his family became members of the 210 Assembly of God Church. Therefore, our entire family of twenty were members of 210 Assembly of God Church. The entire household wanted to serve the Lord, but only God knew their hearts. Most of them were baptized in water. We were happy and blessed for what God had done.

I really thought that was it, but three days later, a mother and two children came asking for help. They were homeless, and I felt in my heart that I could not turn them away, even though we already had twenty. I asked them to wait while I consulted with my wife and the housemother. Both my wife and the housemother agreed that we could take them in. When I told the homeless mother that we could take them in, she began to cry. Again, my heart bubbled over for what we were doing. Now we had twenty children and three adults. Pastor Benjamin oversaw that ministry; she managed all monies and took care of all business concerns.

Our investment in the kingdom of God was great. I thanked God daily for my wife. She collaborated closely with me and never complained about investing into God's kingdom.

I thought that our purpose was complete with the children, and things were settling down with the children's home. Then I heard God telling me to start a radio broadcast. We called it *The Bible Speaks*. This was where we started our next investment: a radio broadcast station in Guyana.

We recorded our messages here in the US with the help of a brother in Christ, Maurice Quick. I would go to his home in the Bronx, New York, where Maurice would do a few weeks of broadcasts for a small fee. The broadcasts were then sent to Guyana, South America, and aired every Wednesday evening at 6:00 p.m. for one hour. To God be the glory. We received testimonies from many that were blessed by the broadcast, *The Bible Speaks*. Every so often, I would ask Pastor Benjamin to speak, and she would go on air live directly from the station.

I received plenty of mail here in the USA from Guyana, South America. One day, I received a telephone call from one of the listeners, Wenneth Chapman, who lived in Berbice, Guyana. She informed me that many people would gather in one place to listen to the broadcast. She wanted to know if there was a *Bible Speaks* ministry in Berbice, Guyana.

I informed her that I had never been to Berbice; therefore, we did not have a ministry there. With excitement in her voice, she asked me to visit her the next time we were in Guyana. My wife and I had already planned to go to Georgetown, Guyana, in July 1999, so we accepted her invitation. We took six of the oldest children that were in the children's home with us. They were so excited to be going to Berbice, they were up early the next day, calling us at the hotel (where my wife and I were staying) to pick them up. We rented a van and picked up the children.

When we arrived at the West Coast of Berbice, we had to take a ferryboat to cross the river to the other side of Berbice River. My wife and I were on the first deck while the children went to the second deck. We had just begun to enjoy the ride across the river when we heard the children crying out, "Uncle! Uncle!" As they called me, I could hear the fear in their voices. Simultaneously, they all called me, saying, "A man is trying to kill himself!"

The man was at the bow of the ferry. I ran down to the bow of the ship and tried to talk to this man, who was of indigenous descent, from jumping over. He told me that his people were calling him and that he had to go. He jumped from the bow of the ship, in front of where the children were sitting, and committed suicide.

That was our first trip to Berbice, and it should have been enough to make us return to Georgetown. Nevertheless, we continued.

When we arrived at Wenneth Chapman's home, we were introduced to some lovely Christian ladies who really loved Jesus. We told them of our encounter on the ship and listened to their concerns as they told us how so many people were being blessed by *The Bible Speaks*. As we continued in conversation, I had genuinely believed in my heart that it was God's plan for us to be there. After our meeting, it was agreed that a church under Abundant Life Ministries Guyana would be established at the home of Wenneth Chapman.

After leaving Berbice, we spent two weeks with our girls at the children's home in Georgetown before returning to New York.

By the year 2000, the church had thirty members when we returned to Berbice. That year, we rented a tent and held a tent service, which ran for one month. The tent meetings were great. Many people accepted Jesus Christ as their Savior. After that month of meetings, the membership had grown to forty-six, and the visitors were so many that we could no longer hold services in Wenneth Chapman's home. Therefore, we rented the tent for another five months. Thank God, it was summertime all year round.

Guyana has either rain or sunshine. The temperature was always in the eighties. At the end of the year 2000, I realized that we would have to purchase a building. Before returning to the States (NY), my wife and I discussed the possibilities. We looked at a building that we thought would be good for our children's home in Berbice and the church, so we inquired about it. We were told that the owner was asking 7,000,000 in Guyana currency (G$)—which is $35,000 for the building. My wife and I decided first that we should acknowledge God before making a final decision.

After fasting and praying, I felt led by God and suggested to my wife that we should refinance our home mortgage in New York and purchase the home in Berbice, Guyana. She agreed and by the grace of God, we did just that. By March 2001, we had purchased the building located at 38 Vryman's Erven NA, Berbice, which is our home for girls, and our church assembly is downstairs. We have since borrowed from the Bank of Guyana G$2,000,000 (which is $10,000 US) to extend the property. We had a Bible school where Pastor Enid Benjamin was the dean of the school. We also had a lunch program where we fed over a hundred children each school day. We continued this program for eight years.

Sister Chapman was ordained as pastor. And we lost one of our great workers who was also a good friend, sister, and minister—Rita Fraser, who went home to be with the Lord in 2013. She is missed. Minister Fraser was a holy and sanctified woman who did not stand for foolishness. She was honest and did not like dishonesty.

During the early part of our ministry in Berbice, during our tent meetings, we met a woman of God, Evangelist Maylene McKenzie, who ministered under the tent. Many people were saved and received the baptism of the Holy Spirit. We needed a pastor at that time because of the growth of our ministry, and we were led to ask her to become the pastor of our Berbice church. We could see the evidence as God used her in a mighty way after we had purchased the home in Berbice.

Several times during our journey of traveling back and forth for our tent services in Berbice, Guyana, some of the members of the Tabernacle of Prayer street team traveled with me and my wife.

Pastor Clayton Simpson has been a constant co-laborer with me in my travels. He has traveled with me for over fourteen years to Trinidad, Guyana, and Dominica. He slept on the floor because the bed given us was too small, and he chose to give me the bed. As a missionary, Brother Simpson, who was a native of America, would have to fetch water from the outside to bathe or to flush the toilets. Since we promoted a hotel in Berbice, we stayed there.

Every Sunday, our church service was packed, and in 2002, our Bible Institute opened with two classes: Christian Workers and Evangelism, which were taught by Pastor Enid Brotherson-Benjamin. It was a wonderful year!

Our first Bible school graduation was held in 2003. Dr. Clayton Simpson, who was the dean of our Bible school in New York, attended the graduation in Guyana, and over fifty-five students graduated.

In 2004, Pastor Maylene McKenzie started a mission on the West Coast of Berbice, in a village called No. 8 Village under a house. Pastor Simpson and I preached there on many occasions. We were fully responsible for the financials of all ministries of Abundant Life Ministries Guyana. The church at No. 8 Village, West Coast Berbice, was growing year after year. Again, many people were saved and baptized.

In 2004, we were blessed with a piece of property that was given to our ministry at the No. 8 Village by Mr. Keith Pluck. The land was approximately five acres. We praised and thanked God for the land.

After returning to New York, by the grace of God, we began soliciting for the ministry in Guyana. We wrote letters to people whom we knew and people who traveled with us throughout the years and saw the work we were doing in Guyana. Our prayers were heard. First, I received a check from a sister in Christ for $10,000. A few weeks later, we got another check from another sister in Christ for $5,000. My wife and I began to praise and thank God for his goodness, his provision, and his power. We then raised $5,000. And now we had $20,000—which is equivalent to G$4,000,000 in Guyana.

We hired a contractor that blessed us with a price suitable for our budget. The work only cost us $3,000, which is equivalent to G$6,000,000 in Guyana. We sent $2,000, and the church at No. 8 Village raised $8,000. Again, my wife and I raised another $2,000.

Because of God's grace, the church at No. 8 Village is now debt-free. It is indeed a beautiful assembly! The church family were incredibly grateful for what the Lord had done through us. The membership has increased. At the present year (2022), the membership is 150, and they are anticipating extending the building.

I look back in amazement. When the church began under a house, the people of God were called all kinds of names by passersby, such as "coconut-branch church." (They used branches around the downstairs of the house for privacy and to keep the rain out.)

Sister Louralene P. Gouveia—who attended our Bible school at New Amsterdam, Berbice, for three years—is now the pastor of No. 8 Assembly. Pastor Gouveia's daughter, Roshanna, got married on December 2013 and has two children. She was ten years old when the church started, and she is also a pastor. Her son, Royland, was eight years old. He is a minister now and is married with children. There were also two nieces, Delicia (ten years old) and Dacia (eight years old), who are now minsters of the gospel of Jesus Christ. Both are married with children. I had the privilege of officiating two of the children's marriages. To God be the glory.

For the past nine years, the church at No. 8 Village has been blessing the community with forty boxes of food every month with the support of our ministry and friends here in the USA.

The years went by so quickly as we have seen many people in our Berbice ministry, where Pastor Maylene McKenzie was pastoring and Pastor Enid Brotherson-Benjamin was the dean of our Bible school. With the leading of the Holy Spirit, we were able to educate hundreds of people in the Word of God. Every year for five consecutive years, the graduates consisted of fifty or more graduating students from our Bible school. There were some from other assemblies, of course.

I thank God for the foundation I got in the Manhattan Bible Institute and the Tabernacle of Prayer for All People Bible Institute. Years later, Pastor Maylene McKenzie of our Berbice church became ill and was no longer able to continue pastoring. One of our graduates, Elder Myrna Samuels, was chosen to take over as pastor of the Berbice ministry.

Our children ministry in Georgetown continued until August of 1998, when the owner of the house we were renting for our children gave us notice that the house was sold, and we had to find somewhere to stay. It was a shock to us, for it was too sudden. We thanked God that he had already given us a home in Berbice, where we were able to take some of our children. The Welfare Department relocated some of the children who could not leave Georgetown, and a few had become adults and were able to support themselves. They did not want to go to Berbice. Mr. and Mrs. Cox found a home for their family. Mr. Cox is now a pastor, and four of their children are musicians, and two are singers with beautiful voices.

What a mighty God we serve. I feel so good in my spirit every time I look back and see what the Lord has done through my wife and me in Guyana.

GOD'S MIRACLE

On November 12, 2018, I was sitting on my bed. It was about seven o'clock in the evening when I had a massive heart attack. My daughter-in-law called 911, and I was out until December 16. I was in a coma.

My daughter, Sharon, and two sons Sheldon and Dwayne told me that I had a heart attack. The ambulance and the police came. They gave me CPR and put me into the ambulance, where I had another heart attack. They then gave me CPR again, and I came back to life a second time.

I was then taken to Winthrop Hospital, where in the emergency room, I had three more heart attacks. This was five heart attacks within one hour. After the fifth attack, the doctor told my wife and children that I was brain-dead, and if they tried to keep me, I would be a vegetable. The doctors brought a form for my wife to sign; however, my wife refused to sign the form. She said, "I am not signing anything."

At that time, all my children and my wife were crying. My wife decided to go into the emergency room where I was lying on a bed. She saw that I was naked. My wife said to the doctor and nurses, "Why do you have my husband exposed like this? Cover him up."

The nurses rushed and found a sheet, covered my body, and took me up to the ICU. While I was in a coma, I knew nothing. I was told that while I was in the ICU, I had a cardiac arrest, and once again, the doctor came to my wife and told her and my children that there was nothing more he could do. Once again, he gave them a form to sign. My daughter-in-law Nigel Johnson, with a stern voice, said, "We are not signing anything. He is in God's hand."

The doctor ordered them to place me on ice. I was told that I was on a bed covered with ice for eight days. My daughter and Samantha took turns sleeping in the waiting room for one week.

While I was in a coma, it was like a dream where I found myself at the bottom of a river or ocean. On my right side, I saw a bright light. Out of the light came a voice saying, "You shall not die but live. Warn my people. I am coming, coming for my church. I am coming for my church." And the voice began fading and said, "I am coming for my church." And then the light disappeared.

After my eighth day on ice, the ice was removed. I was told that the purpose of having me on ice was to try to preserve my brain and organs. There were many people there when they removed the ice: Pastor Barbara Mitchell, Sister Desire Forde, Pastor William Johashen, and other pastors and friends along with my children and wife. For the final time, the doctor told my family and all the people that were with them that there was nothing more they could do for me.

At that time, everyone was crying, including the pastors. Then my son Dwayne held my toe and said, "Dad, I know you can hear me. If you do, wiggle your toe."

At that time, though in a coma, I heard those words. I was told that my left foot went up in the air. At that time, the doctors who were there realized that I was not brain-dead and began to treat me accordingly.

Praise the Lord. He is a miracle-working God. I came out of the coma a few days later and was kept one more week in the hospital. My wife did not leave my side; she stayed in a chair, sleeping next to me.

On December 25, I was sent to a rehab center, where I spent Christmas. While in the rehab center, it was difficult because I had to use a walker, and there were too many elderly people that made me uncomfortable. I asked the doctor to let me go home for the New Year to be with my family. They granted my request, but I was only allowed one day.

When I returned the next day, I told the doctor I would like to go home. I was then told that I could not be discharged because my treatments had three more weeks before completion. I felt that I could not take being surrounded by so many seniors aged ninety and above, some crying and acting out all night. The next morning, I told the doctor that I would like to sign myself out. Every day, I would ask the doctor to let me sign myself out of the rehab, and I would get the same answer: "No, you are not ready."

Then, finally, one day, he said, "Okay, you can go home."

I said, "Thank God."

My son Dexter picked me up. I was happy to be back home and in my own bed. The following week, I joined an outpatient therapy. I was there for one month. God did wonders through the therapist who was assigned to me.

On April 1, 2019, I went to the ICU Department at Winthrop Hospital to thank the nurses and doctors. I met the doctor who, on two occasions, told my family that there was nothing more that could be done for me and was encouraging them to sign a form to release me. Thank God they did not sign.

The nurses were happy to see me, and they began calling me the "miracle man." I had to tell them the Miracle Man was Jesus Christ. He gets all the glory. Many of the pastors and friends told me that it was the first miracle they had ever witnessed.

God is still in the miracle-working business. He brought me back for a purpose! Amen.

A Letter to Everyone Who Has Read This Book

I thank each of you for taking the time to read my book. On this twenty-sixth day of January 2022, I give all the praise to my Lord and Savior Jesus Christ for allowing me to see this day. I am now eighty-one years old, and if the Lord allows me to see June 12, 2022, I will be eighty-two.

God is an awesome God. He loved me so much that He sent Jesus Christ, His Son, to pay that price on the cross to redeem me—not only me but the entire world. When I think of the love of Jesus Christ, it makes me want to shout "Hallelujah!" Only God can bring a person, whose life was in the pit, to a place of princes, "having predestined us unto the adoption of children by Jesus Christ Himself according to the good pleasure of his will" (Ephesians 1:5). We are made children of God when we repent of our sins and accept Christ as our Savior. We then become his children, "being confident of this very thing, that he which has begun a good work in you will perform it until the day of Jesus Christ [the Rapture]" (Philippians 1:6).

My friends and family of God, he is no respecter of persons. What God has done for me, he can do for any other child of God. Your faith in action brings results. So I pray that everyone who has read this book, if you do not know Jesus Christ as your Lord and Savior, you would make that decision today.

The rapture of the church is near. We do not know the day or time, but we do know he is coming. That was what I was told by God.

May the blessings of God be with each of you. *Jesus Christ is coming soon.*

Forever Grateful,
Apostle Roderick Johnson

About the Author

Apostle Roderick is a man of God—a man after God's heart who genuinely loves God and the work that God assigned to him. He never allows adversity, sickness, or money issues to slow him down or stop him. He is like a lion with the strength of an ox. Apostle Johnson truly is called and predestined by God to do the work that he was chosen to do. He worked his regular job, but when it came to God's work, he did not let anything stand in his way. When he was not feeling well in his body, no one knew because he would continue to press on, standing on God's Word (Isaiah 53:5).

Apostle Roderick Johnson believes that there are souls assigned to him and is determined to reach every soul at any cost. He would always say "duty calls" and "souls are waiting to be saved." He would let nothing separate him from the love he has for God and his people. He knew people would be waiting to be fed spiritually, physically, and mentally.

Apostle Roderick Johnson is totally submitted to God and committed to the kingdom's work. He wants to win souls for the kingdom because he knows that winning souls is wise.

Because of Christ,
Clayton Simpson

www.ingramcontent.com/pod-product-compliance
Lightning Source LLC
Chambersburg PA
CBHW021142130726
47988CB00003B/1426